Constant Traffic

poems by

Justin Paige

Finishing Line Press
Georgetown, Kentucky

Constant Traffic

Copyright © 2017 by Justin Paige
ISBN 978-1-63534-258-1 First Edition
All rights reserved under International and Pan-American Copyright Conventions.
No part of this book may be reproduced in any manner whatsoever without written permission from the publisher, except in the case of brief quotations embodied in critical articles and reviews.

ACKNOWLEDGMENTS

You—you know who you are, reader—the one in my head, the one in my heart, the one everywhere and nowhere, everyone and no one, the one, the many, the real, the idea, the ideal and the flaws, the fur and the claws

Also Starring: Ralph Angel, Jason Arment, Erin Belieu, Jen Bervin, Adam Ceserano, Zach Cioffi, Mark Cox, Carla Criscuolo, Dewey Lounge, Finishing Line Press, FSU, Michael Gagliardi, Jody Gladding, JonLouis Gonzalez, Paul Guernsey, Daniel Hammer, Richard Jackson, David Kirby, Daniel McGinn, Miami, Devin Paige, Michele Paige, Mary Ruefle, Daniel Schneider, The Stenders, VCFA, David Wojahn, ZBT

Publisher: Leah Maines

Editor: Christen Kincaid

Cover Art: JonLouis Gonzalez

Author Photo: Melanie Gabrielle

Cover Design: Elizabeth Maines McCleavy

Printed in the USA on acid-free paper.
Order online: www.finishinglinepress.com
        also available on amazon.com

Author inquiries and mail orders:
Finishing Line Press
P. O. Box 1626
Georgetown, Kentucky 40324
U. S. A.

Table of Contents

Flight Attendants, Prepare for Arrival 1
Parallelogram 2
Passersby 4
Television Meditation 6
Rusted Hammock Hooks 7
Instructions were made to be trashed 9
The Dichotomy 11
Morning's Not Meant for Tap-Dancing 12
Floral Arrangements 13
Breath of your air 15
Developer fee 16
Constant Traffic 18
Lifecycle 19
Sands of time 20
Beach song 21
Consider Me Loony 22
Song with stagnation 23
Map of the liberated state 24
Homage to Asian Allegories 25
Winemaking for Dummies 26
A dandelion less delicate than time 27
Drive-by 28
Careful of the upsell 29
How Does the Gloss Taste? 30
Why I Want to Be an Ancient Egyptian 31
Man's Best Teacher 32

"They say the universe is expanding.
That should help with the traffic."

—Steven Wright

Flight Attendants, Prepare for Arrival

The wake-up cue
raises the curtains
on cityscape lights—
thousands of lighthouses
guiding a safe return.

But why do I think
of jagged rocks
and see man's story—
his cunning craft
and all that have fallen
in its wake?

Each light overpowers
the dark and turns
into a trophy; spotlights
a population expanding
to keep up with technology
like a jealous neighbor—
an armrest-stealing row-mate
with their seat affixed back.

Yet the people below
or onboard aren't flying
kites in thunderstorms
or sailing to new worlds;
they're waiting

to take us
in their arms;
sigh at our late flight
and their hungry dog;
bump us as they rush
out the aisle;
catch our attention
from the corner of our eye;
smirk and turn away
or embrace
an opportunity.

Parallelogram

Should we pity
parallel lines—
heading the same direction
every day, side-by-side
on the highway, never veering
off the same exit,
experiencing the connection
in coincidence,
defying the odds together
at adjoining gas pumps?

Do they ever glare
through windows, wave,
blow kisses or long
to crash
into the other car
to force an introduction?

That would beat living
like two people
arriving in the same building
every morning,
spotting each other
in the parking lot
and slipping
into separate offices.

Perhaps parallel lines
are happily ignorant;
they don't intersect
once and grow
eternally apart or
wreck a chance
encounter in the elevator
and press every button
to exit any floor.

Parallel lines don't worry
about other drivers
and can focus on the road
and dial in their iPods.
They could give a flying parabola
about running into
their life-long partner,
content to have someone
along for the ride.

Passersby

Sometimes your eyes meet
across the bar, and you smile,
but don't look again.
It's easier that way;
it's less complicated.

You can imagine intimacy,
in other words,
like the fellowship founded
with the driver who tips you off
to the cop waiting
in the median
or the eye contact
with others in line
that validates
the clerk's ineptitude.

It's the knowing look
shared with dog owners
scooping up
their civic duties
or with a sports fan
wearing the same jersey
in hostile territory.

But this sports bar is loud
and too cramped
to even see the TVs.
So maybe you rush
to the door and leave
the bouncer holding it
nothing but dutiful thanks,
while the door you long for
opens for more

and justifies
all the strangers
we let in.

Television Meditation

It starts during something
mindless, like watching TV,
before I cast characters
as their real-world
counterparts, attach
to their stories
and skip plans
to tune in, though
they follow
my predictions and replay
ad nauseam.

Even memories become stories
I tell myself
and recite to others,
like that time at camp
I first kissed
the girl who finally
said yes to the dance
when we came close,
our lips pulsing
to the beat, the room spinning, blurring
other dancers, bending
light in our reflection.

She was actually
the only girl
I asked the prior night,
after she cried
in an empty room,
and my last partner
until college, where
I learned to approach
and got the courage
to touch hips.

Rusted Hammock Hooks

I am a beach hammock
        looking to swing away
                your worries,
sand   passing
        through your toes   and kicked
                from your flip flops.

I am the goo
        beneath your beagle's eyelid
                that you must wipe
                      away every day.

I am the headlights
        you search for
                on a deserted interstate.

I am the deserted interstate.
                      I am not the headlights.

Nor am I the switch   you seek
                while stumbling
                      through the dark.

I am the single bulb,
        flickering
                  once you reach
                      the stairs.

I am chills   on a cold night
                in Nothingness, Nebraska,
                      but I am not your blanket.

I am not wrapped around you,
                        breathed in   with roses and baby food.
I am not the thought
                            grasped before sleep;
                            recited in your nightly prayer;
                            seated at your breakfast table.

I am waking up   for work
                    every morning   and saving you
                                  from a burning building
                                      on my way home.

I am in no need
                of news coverage.
                    I only need   some wind
                            to push us along.

Instructions were made to be trashed

I live in a high-rise,
        on the third floor.
               From my balcony I see   (and hear)
                          the traffic—
        automotive and human.   I watch and listen
                        to both rev and screech.
The cars' intent's easier
        to understand; their signals
                clearer (though not always
                      louder). The people
                      at restaurants below
                         become noise—
their murmurs cloud together,
        the clanging of their silverware
                more identifiable
                      than a voice in the crowd.

So I listen   (and look)
        for Ferraris,   planes
            flying overhead
                or the slight sway
                of eye-level palm trees.
And I turn away
    from low-cut dresses,
            afraid   the upturned eyes
                    might catch mine.

(I had to go   to the bathroom, anyway.)
                There I stand and pee neon yellow—
                        my ode
                        to vitamin B2
and its promotion
        of energy metabolism or
                      something.

Mostly it lets me remember
                I had my multi and probiotic
                              and maintained   my body's
                                                    daily health.

But why don't I   disobey
                        the one-a-day   directions?

I want to overdose
                    on nutrients.

No,
      I want to grab
           the open bottle,
                        listen   to the pills rattle,
                              and guess   the amount
                                  I fling over the balcony

            and watch
                fall
                        into the cleavage
                                of the blonde below.

The Dichotomy

I want to argue with you
that being lost assumes a destination,

which we can never reach
if we keep going   halfway,

according to Zeno's paradox.
I want you to spin square circles,

retort that you and I
are infinitely   divisible

and send me
                        to the other side of the universe
then remind me of entanglement
            where even our quarks   are vines
                                entwined
                                      across the galaxy
I want to man a NASA Voyager
        to explore every planet
                in our solar system
                        then go interstellar
revering silence
        while reaching   the next star system
                        and its universal lessons
until I want to just be
      with you and build
             a teleportation device
                   that beams me to you
                        so my particles weave with yours
before our bodies reassemble
      and even if we embrace
                    our atoms   never   touch

Morning's Not Meant for Tap-Dancing

I know to tiptoe
in the wee hours
while others sleep.
The trick's to slowly
lift my feet,
or skin sticks
to the floor
and flicks others
awake before
I make my daily escape.

My dog's the first to stir
on any heavy footstep,
joining me in the kitchen,
jingling her tags,
joyfully announcing
her hope for a walk
before I finish my breakfast.

I know to tiptoe
so I don't feel guilty
about rousing my girlfriend,
seeing her squirm
and kick off sheets
before muttering
something from her dreams.

I know to tiptoe.

Floral Arrangements

What do flowers say, anyway?
Tulips gossip
and reminisce about
the glory days
of their mania
while solemnly recognizing
all things that boom
must bust.
(Did that communicate
the concept of invaluableness?)

Orchids morbidly
tell widows to forget
the water
and let them wilt
beside the urn.
(Is that empathy?)

Roses seduce,
lulling in pickers
with red coats concealing
their pricks beneath.
Or maybe their sweet scent
reveals that names matter
and one only transcends expectations
through death.
(Does that mean beauty transcends?)

Sunflowers scoff
at Van Gogh
and turn up their noses
to the sun god.

(Is it cliché to suggest
greatness goes unnoticed
by the masses?)

Dandelions pray
to blow away,
no, for the moment
when their florets
can travel anywhere.
(Own the cliché,
say that moment exists
whenever with you.)

Touch-me-nots plead
for a touch
to send them inward.
(Say it, that after
their deepest droop
they bloom brighter
because of your touch.)

Breath of your air

In this room
without you
Windows
stick shut
Vents
cough dust
without you

With you
windows
crack
breeze blows through
with sun's shine
birds' chirps
and I
I breathe
breathe in
you

You
crack
the sun
inhale the breeze
exhale gales
let birds glide
and I
I breathe
breathe in

Developer fee

Bird chirps stir the trees from sleep
Soot battles roots
as bulldozers' fumes loom
from the birds' perch   muzzling
their tweets

Chippers approach
the trunks with axes
and scurry
the birds on every
strike

Strikes
resound among the remaining
trees   trembling
from the tractors
rumbling closer

Closer
they lurch and
crumble branches
under their tracks—
every crack

snaps
awareness
of the trees and
ants marching
snakes crawling

deer trotting
somewhere
seeking
food   shade   terrain
to run

Bird chirps stir
flutter to the heavens
entreat the flock to follow
to wires spotted
in the sprouting city

Constant Traffic

Ants crawl through the cracks
to share my breakfast
and clean the counter.
I squash them
with a dish rag
and spray insecticide
that guarantees
one-year protection.
If only it were that easy—
cockroaches squeeze
through the cracks
of my mind and hide
under the armoire
when I hunt
them. Moths cloud
the light I flick on
to crack
the darkness.

Caterpillars
are caterpillars
until their cocoons crack.
Branches crack
not from the weight
of the ants,
but from their constant
traffic—the same
persistence that traverses
walls. My head cracks
open on the armoire
and a butterfly escapes
and flutters past
the moths to find
the cracks
of light.

Lifecycle

Stuck in the rain, no,
not like an expression, like
a truck in mud
spinning its wheels
digging deeper
with every rev
as I try to break free
by running, not
like a slave, more like a bird
that overslept
and missed the V.

Pedal toward blue skies
in sight, clouded by rain
on my glasses and
clouds forming
when I get closer
and drizzle turns
to downpour,
like depression. Give up
and head home,
not like a defeated army,
like a kid kicked out
of the sandbox.

Home in the box,
A/C like a Miami condo
blasting, yes, like a barrage
of microscopic ice bullets piercing
until jumping in the shower, yes,
literally, yes, hot water, yes, oh yes.
And how those bullets melt, no,
not to say storms pour
appreciation of clear skies or
rainbows, just to say,
damn, that feels good.

Sands of time

Once stone,
which could kill
two birds or skip
along the ocean,
worn away
wave after wave

separating every sediment,
leaving speckles of itself
that, after eons of change,
end up kicked through flip flops,
cursed when found in underwear.

Or maybe stone—
no longer
weighed down,
thrown and used
to kill—

frees itself
as sand and sees
the shores
from Normandy to Miami,
where families build
castles in its honor
and welcome it home.

Beach song

The waves whoosh and crash
whoosh
and crash
and begin to build
from afar
rolling along
pushing fish from the deep
while pelicans hover above
waiting
watching
listening
to waves whoosh
and crash
until ready
to dive
and snatch the fish
swimming through my mind

Consider Me Loony

Imagine yourself—
a young man at the beach
with a book poised
in front,
eyes intent
on the girls
in your periphery.
You know how
you're unable
to show
you're watching,
how your eyes
stay attached
to the book?

Do you think
this would be like
catching a glimmer
of the world's spectacle
in the corner of your eye
and suppressing
your reaction,
afraid those near
would rather hear
a current event,
game score or
educated guess
of the brunette's cup size?

Would you be found loony
if you began a litany
after looking past the brunette
and seeing the rippling
waves and wondering
about the world's causal nature
and your limited presence
in its grandeur?

Song with stagnation
Response to Federico García Lorca's
"Canción con movimiento" (1860)

Darkening star
sightless
through fluorescent fog
waiting
millions of years
for its light
to beam to earth before
struggling
against the stifling
man-made glare

Disappearing star
hidden
in its empty corner
of the galaxy
until
shining among
a barren patch of land
where a man sits
looking up
wondering
his universal role

Map of the liberated state

A tour guide told me
               as we traversed   a maze
                                   of side streets
                            and cramped crowds
and discovered a quiet spot
                       in Venice

that sometimes   you need
                       to get lost
                             to find yourself,

and my mind
              wandered,
                       leaving the city
                                 without a water taxi.

How are packed people
         any different from gnawing neurons
              firing boisterous obligations,
                   marble facades reminding
                                of bills due?

Do we really need a map
              to find the nearest catedral
                             or a tour guide to tell us
St. Mark's was built in 1050
          as a symbol   of the Republic's power
to be knocked
         into consciousness
                    when we find
                             our private entrance?

Homage to Asian Allegories

Sometimes I wish I came from
                      dragons
                                      so I could blow   hot air.

Or I long   for the wooden houses
                      housing the dragon carvings
                                to catch fire
                  and disprove   the legend.

What do koi see
                with their eyes   always   open?
Do silk worms believe
                in the kimono   that takes   their lives?
Why is the crane   a symbol   of longevity?

                                          Because it can
                                                    fly.

A cherry blossom   blooms
        in the water's   reflection,
                reflects   every hand-laborer
                            that labored
                                      for this garden
and shows   a sign
              of the dragon's   protection—
                      350 flame-free years.

Winemaking for Dummies

The vintner plants seeds and waits
for seasons
to harvest his grapes.
He inspects them with soft hands
squeezing their juice
and carefully destems
and crushes them.
Fermentation begins,
and he waits.

Now wine, he transfers them
to barrels and waits.
He bottles them
and waits.
He labels them
a vintage he sells
to a connoisseur
who places them on his rack
and waits.

A dandelion less delicate than time

A plucked dandelion demands
to be blown—
                to free its florets
in wind's   randomness

they hope will propel
                      them beyond
                      the blower's eyes and
breath.   But what about
                a dandelion not blown?

Eyes and breath
                extinguish. Only
limitless
        florets and wind's

                randomness
remain,   ready
            to travel   anywhere.

Drive-by

The tree-lined street leads
to safety and shades
the quaint neighborhood
from stray
bullets a few blocks away.

Moss drops
on the car of the couple
who drive through
and revere wrought iron
that rivals
the roots' history.

They eye trimmed
hedges, say that signifies
the pride needed
to ground a community
and deride the roads passed
filled with trash and cracks

while the smooth path
guides them quietly back
past the immaculate facades
with owners watching
through impact-proof windows.

But the pavement breaks
jostle their car
and draw attention
to people outside
on their couches watching
a kid as he rifles

through rummage,
finds a pipe he holds high
as a scepter and runs
to his friends waiting
with a tin-foil ball.

Careful of the upsell

Salvation's free with
a weekly contribution,
like the tip
for my dance, the stripper asks, or
lifelong love for
a diamond and house.

All I wanted
was an all-you-can-eat brunch,
not a pay-per-cup coffee,
and now I'm likening strippers
to religion and marriage, not sure
which is more offensive.

Depends on whom you ask
or depends on the salesman.
Maybe it's true—
the stripper's paying for college,
the church needs a new steeple,
she loves you.

But some car salesmen salivate
at the thought of adding clear coat
and blot those that dutifully do
and lose themselves
in figures and horsepower,
forgetting the drivers—

no different from Heisenberg
after strings of sleepless nights
consumed by a problem
to solve. So I guess the question is
who creates the bomb
and why I want more
than one cup of coffee.

How Does the Gloss Taste?

When sacrificing a life
becomes nothing more
than passing the potatoes,
a reader quickly takes interest.

But our 21st century audience
turned empathy off
after the news.
They aren't severing
their viscera to show
the chief their dedication
and one up their tribesman,
who could only cut off his ear.

Sure, you can write
and write and write,
but will you
accept your fate—
your ultimate resignation
to a supreme power,
via church, state,
or anything between?

Or will you just question
adherence to a flimsy system;
be reminded
of Van Gogh's passion;
or envision
the sanguine tubular unfolding
as intestines spill?

Why I Want to Be an Ancient Egyptian

You might expect me to envy
a pharaoh's divinity—
his God-like rule
over worshipping followers—
or for Midas
to turn my mind to gold
and raid the tombs from thought.

But I want to be a laborer—
one of the countless toiling
all day over one stone,
each at my side piling
on the stone's tonnage
with every speck of sweat;
each quarter-step
bringing us beyond
the skies we study.

For a trip to Egypt taught
it was not the whip
that built these wonders.
Most worked unbound
by slaves' shackles
because their belief
of defeating death
through pyramids' after-life.

And I want that feeling.
No, I don't long
for immortality,
but I seek
that conviction
in anything.

Man's Best Teacher

At a Puerto Rican plaza
a group gathered
around a skeleton
of a dog or rat
with xylophone ribs.
Someone gave

a slab of meat
bigger than he,
which he slowly
licked—each tongue-full
adding a minute of life.
Another, worried

the piece too big,
tried to extract
and cut it for him—
for a few more days,
alleys and starving pleas
at restaurants' backdoors

and kicks from frustrated owners.
But when they tried,
the dog fought
his gentle nature, scowled,
snatched the meat,
chewed what he could
and swallowed it whole.

Justin began writing poetry while studying creative writing at Florida State University and desiring a way to delve further into characters and ideas from his stories and novels (no longer) in progress. After moving past short stories with random enjambments and aureate verbiage, he started to see some things possible in words and forms, while mostly trapped in exposition and predetermined ideas (read: conceits). Through constant experimentation and assistance during his MFA at Vermont College, he learned to let language and form guide the work and found enlightening moments when he was lost, but the poem was aware. "Constant Traffic" covers part of this journey, along with actual journeys through his job in the tourism industry.

Justin's work appears in numerous corporate communications. He hopes poetry one day puts air beneath his wings, but he sometimes suffers from clichés and cynicism while living, working and occasionally writing in Miami.

www.ingramcontent.com/pod-product-compliance
Lightning Source LLC
LaVergne TN
LVHW041600070426
835507LV00011B/1206